All the Best!

Ann Ouellette

Classic Creole:

A Celebration of Food and Family

Ann Cuiellette

Southeast Missouri State University Press • 2011

Classic Creole: A Celebration of Food and Family

ISBN: 978-0-9830504-0-7

First published in the United States of America, 2011.

Southeast Missouri State University Press
One University Plaza, MS 2650
Cape Girardeau, MO 63701
http://www6.semo.edu/universitypress

Cover design by Aaron Purnell, Creative Highway
http://www.creativehighwaydesign.com

Cover and food photography by Steve Adams

Acknowledgments

This book is dedicated to my husband Craig and my two daughters, Eve and Mia. Thank you for your neverending support, love, and encouragement. When I think about my life, I cannot imagine being in this world without all of you. Craig, you are my soulmate, and every day I thank God that I found you. Your unending love and devotion has touched my life deeply, and your compassion and humor has made all of our lives joyous. Thanks for being my "greatest fan"!

Eve and Mia, I adore you both, and I love you more than words can describe. I thank you both for your inspiration and life-long memories. It has been a pleasure to watch you grow into beautiful young women. I am so proud of you. I thank you for staying true to your own passions. You both possess extraordinary talents and gifts, and I will always be here to cheer you on. Thanks for your love and support.

I would also like to acknowledge my five sisters Jennifer, Denise, Rhonda, Donna, and Eleanor. Thanks for your guidance throughout my life and for giving me the unconditional gift of love each and every day. You have all been amazing role models. I will forever appreciate and cherish the bond of sisterhood and your constant presence in my life.

To my brothers—Gerald, Byron, Rene, Keith, Kenneth, Eric, and Alvarez. Thanks for your fun-loving spirit, your passion for family, and for "keeping it real." To my cousin and closest confidant, Shayne, I delight in our childhood memories together and all the special times we spent together. Thank you for your neverending support, loyalty, and friendship.

To my best friends—Peggy Newman, Mary Elizabeth Bunzel, Geri Charbonnet Clifton, and Arnold Donald. Great friends in this world are so rare. I am lucky to have found you all. I will forever cherish your individual gifts and how you have each been a part of my life over the years.

To my father and mother (Rene and Baylissa)—I think of you both every day of my life. I am grateful for your caring, incredible family legacy, humanity, and how you raised thirteen children in a warm, loving household. I am forever guided by your spirit. The legacy of our family continues to inspire me. Thank you for the gift of life and everlasting memories.

Special thanks to photographer, Steve Adams. Your ability to capture the essence of the food in these photographs is amazing, and you did an outstanding job in making me look great! I thank you for your tireless efforts, brilliant vision, and friendship to me and Craig.

To my nephew, Aaron Purnell, thanks for creating an amazing cover. You are truly a gifted artist, and your creativity and talent will take you very far.

Susan Swartwout, thanks for your support, vision, and enthusiasm about this project. I appreciate your insights and ability to bring this book to life. I will always remember how you believed in me and my quest to honor my family heritage.

About the Author

Ann Cuiellette, a native of New Orleans, grew up in a large, Creole family as the twelfth of thirteen children. Ann holds a bachelor's degree in Human Resource Management from Webster University in St. Louis and is currently a business executive for a technology company.

I loved being in the kitchen with my mother, and I absorbed all her passion for cooking as well as her art for entertaining. All the dishes I cook are authentic New Orleans family recipes from my mother and grandmother but certainly updated to reflect my own flare for cooking. I have always had a lifelong passion for cooking and entertaining. Over twelve years ago I was involved in a charity event, but as a way to offer something different, a friend asked me to auction off a Creole dinner to support the organization. This gave me a chance to support the charity, but also an opportunity to cook and bring New Orleans food to others, right in the privacy of their own home! I met lots of great people and, of course, they loved the food!

After Hurricane Katrina hit New Orleans, which was a personal devastation for me, I decided to write a cookbook entitled "Classic Creole." I wanted the recipes that I love so much to be available to share with others as a way to honor my family heritage. But it's not just a cookbook—it's a "storybook"; each recipe has a brief note about my experience eating that dish as I was growing up.

The city I love is still recovering from the devastation of Hurricane Katrina. Thank you for your interest in the continuing story of New Orleans families who are recovering from the lasting effects of this tragedy.

Table of Contents

If the Spice Is Right

When you think about New Orleans, you can close your eyes and smell the aroma of gumbo, etoufee, or the lingering scent of boiled seafood. Their spices and their authentic smells are what make the Crescent City so unique. My mother believed that well-seasoned food was essential in bringing a dish alive. But she was adamant about using two basic ingredients—salt and pepper. Well-seasoned food made all the difference in the outcome of the dish and ultimately the finished product, she said. If the "spice is right," you will have the best results. Listed below are some essential spices for authentic New Orleans cooking:

Salt & Pepper – This is the most important ingredient you will use. Don't be stingy; be generous, and it will bring the flavor of your dishes to life.

Creole Seasoning – Tony Chachere's Creole seasoning is a combination of salt, red pepper, garlic, and other spices. This is a staple in any Creole kitchen.

Gumbo Filé – This is an American-Indian spice made up from the leaves of the sassafras tree. This unique, aromatic flavor is used for gumbo and soups.

Thyme – Used in soups, gumbo, and sauces.

Rosemary – Great flavor for chicken, lamb, and potatoes.

Seafood Boil – A packet of spices used for boiling seafood (crab, crawfish, shrimp), which contains mustard seed, coriander seed, cayenne pepper, bay leaves, dill seeds, cloves, and allspice. The scent will knock your socks off!

Tabasco Sauce – This is present in every household and restaurant in New Orleans and adds just the right amount of "kick" to any dish.

Garlic – Good for the heart and keeps the vampires away.

Onions – Yellow onions, sweet and delicious.

Bay Leaves – Enhances the flavors of soups, sauces, and just about every New Orleans dish.

Roux – Foundation of sauces. A mixture of flour, butter, and oil.

Introduction

"Do you know what it means to Miss New Orleans?"

New Orleans is in my blood. No matter where I live in this world I will always call it home. If you spend five minutes talking to me, it is clear where I come from and how proud I am to be a descendent of this great city. The uniqueness of the city can also be summed up by the trifecta of the waters that surround the city—the Gulf of Mexico, the Mississippi River, and Lake Pontchartrain. Since the city is below sea level, there are also countless bayous, canals, and waterways that circle the state. This unique combination, and the prominent French influence, prompts so many to refer to New Orleans as a European city right here in the United States. When you visit New Orleans you are mesmerized by the culture, the architecture, the cobblestone streets, the sidewalk cafes, the music, and the people, but most importantly you are seduced by the decadent aroma of the food. The food stays in your memories long after you leave the Crescent City; its flavors linger in the air like a cloud. You can't quite identify each individual ingredient, but this special combination of flavors produces a culinary dining experience you will always remember.

After the devastation of Hurricane Katrina, I was compelled to bring the wonderful recipes of my family to life. These recipes are unique and authentically "Creole." When I reminisce about the foods of my past, I think about the history of my family and the experience I had with each dish as I was growing up. Along with each of these wonderful recipes, I bring to you my family story, filled with passion, rich with history, and sprinkled with fun.

New Orleans is a place where food has always been the center of attention; food is not just for nourishment but it is a way of life for dwellers of the city. When you step off a plane or out of a car, you smell an aroma of flavors and spices so alluring that you head directly to the nearest restaurant to embark on your journey through the bounties of seafood and beverages you yearn to explore. You begin this journey knowing that you will always be enticed to return over and over again. Maybe your reason to visit was to experience the madness of Mardi Gras, but once you drink from the fountain that is New Orleans, you will always be back. Come and share my experiences and how this food played such an important part in my family's history.

I was born the twelfth of thirteen children in a traditional New Orleans Creole household. Both of my parents were the oldest in their families; my mother was the oldest of five and my father had two younger siblings. My parents loved being with family and friends, and they enjoyed entertaining. In addition to our immediate family, we always seemed to have others gather around the table for dinner or just to be a part of the party-like atmosphere that existed at our house. And, in traditional New Orleans style, food was the center of everything.

Growing up in this large family was an integral part of who I am today. The warmth, love, compassion, and camaraderie were exhilarating, and there was never a dull moment. A common spirit of energy and enthusiasm thrived among my siblings, and we were all very close, despite age or gender. Each and every person who stepped across our threshold was welcomed into a home like they had never seen before. Excitement, vitality, and stimulating conversations filled the house at every turn. Holidays were especially fun because that meant more people but also more delicious food.

My mother was tall and slim. Her charming and captivating personality was evident to guests immediately. She was the quintessential entertainer and brought great style and elegance to any occasion. Her warmth and accessibility made her endearing to everyone she met; her blue eyes always twinkled, while her silver hair shone like fine steel. She lost her mother when she was twelve, but took great responsibility in helping her father raise her younger siblings. My grandfather owned a very successful insurance company and had a high regard for education. In those days (1920s and 1930s), Creole families settled in the Seventh Ward, an area in the city populated with well-educated and highly skilled individuals. This area of the city was very progressive, and families thrived while the city continued to expand. So many things were happening in the city during that time, and the combination of up-and-coming successful entrepreneurs, coupled with educated Creoles, gave way to a prosperous era.

My mother was from a very aristocratic Creole family—descendents of "Creole Royalty," a phrase I heard throughout my life and still today—and we are all proud of that distinction. While not a lot of specifics are known about this "royal family," there was no arguing the point about my mother's heritage. My grandfather's family made the journey to Louisiana from the Dominican Republic, where we were told their French family of "kings and queens" were kicked out of this tiny little town to make room for the Spanish. In any event, we were obliged to accept our fate and wore it proudly like a badge of honor.

My mother was an advocate of education and wanted all of her children to appreciate the power of knowledge. She attended one of the first high schools in New Orleans for African Americans and went on to Xavier University, a prominent historical black college in New Orleans. She was always writing or reading something and was very articulate at communicating her thoughts. She also understood how different cultures were important and should be embraced and celebrated. This was something that served us well.

Our family legacy was also deeply rooted in our connection to the great Voodoo Queen of New Orleans—Marie Laveau. My great-grandmother, Seliniere Glapion, was one of the offspring of the great Marie Laveau. Of course, not a lot was said about the teachings and practices of voodoo, but we all knew and believed in its existence. Superstitions and traditions were prevalent, and there were times when my mother would create a "cure" for an illness by wrapping herbs in a cheese cloth, dipping it in tea, then placing it under your pillow at night. You accepted the gesture, didn't ask questions about the ritual, and were amazed at the results.

While both my parents were very close to their siblings, back in the 1950s a wave of Creoles left New Orleans for the West Coast. Two of my mother's siblings remained in New Orleans, but Aunt Gwendolyn, or "Nanan," and Uncle George; her youngest sister, Aunt Deannie; brother, Uncle Gerald; and my father's brother, Uncle Wendell, made the pilgrimage to California for better career opportunities, the warmth of the sun, and the cool breeze of the ocean. They all settled in Los Angeles with many other Creole families. Their migration from the South eventually created a mini-New Orleans on the West Coast. Creoles opened grocery stores that sold New Orleans foods, started social clubs, and celebrated their own brand of Mardi Gras. Most of these ventures are still around today. My parents missed their siblings terribly and went to great efforts to stay close to our relatives.

My father grew up in a hard-working family. The Seventh Ward's prosperous businesses made it possible for his family to excel. They came from a long line of skilled laborers who were masters at creating granite and tile work that looked like exquisite renditions of Monet, Picasso, and other masters of art. My father's family and other craftsmen assisted in creating the great halls of many buildings in the New Orleans area. At the end of the day, the calluses on my father's hands were a reminder of his commitment to support his family. My father was strong, rugged, and had a commanding presence, although he was not very tall, and hard work and dedication were the standards he lived by. My father had the most amazing work ethic, promptly awake at five in the morning. He started his day by taking two aspirin (long before it was fashionable), then chased them down with a little Coke every day. This ritual, he believed, was why he never got sick.

My father was in the Great War—World War II—and like most soldiers from that generation, he rarely spoke about his experience in the war. I think he believed that part of his life was private, and although he spent time in Europe and was even wounded, it was not something he spoke about often. However, I do know he was proud of his service to his country.

The contrast of my parents' families was interesting. My mother lost her own mother early in her life, and she was raised by her father. My father's parents divorced when he was young, but he was very close to his mother. When my grandmother came to visit, we all had to be on our best behavior. Little Mother, as we called her, was a tough, no-nonsense woman who worked outside of the home throughout her life, which was very rare in those days. My father was her only son, and although she was tough, she always had a soft spot for him. My father was extremely close to his sister (Aunt Geraldine), and he visited her often, usually coming back from her house with a homemade cake or pie for the family—he loved dessert. My father's only brother (Uncle Wendell) moved out west, but they were in constant contact all through their lives.

My father's family hailed from England and had an incredible background traced back to several generations in New Orleans. A descendent of the Spanish Governor of Louisiana, Bernardo de Galvez, this family legacy was filled with the rich history that makes up so many families in the great city of New Orleans. As a reminder of this part of the history in our family, my grandmother had a rare photo of the Governor and his daughter, etched in glass. This was a family heirloom which now resides with my Aunt Geraldine.

At home both my parents were warm and caring and always made everyone who walked through the doors of our home feel welcome. My mother was an excellent cook, and whenever we sat down for dinner, there was always a guest at the dinner table—a cousin, aunt, uncle, or friend. *There is always room for one more at the table*, she would say. She prepared a different meal every day in very large pots—the kind you see in restaurants. Were there ever any leftovers? Never! When I was growing up, I didn't know what leftovers were because there was never anything left over after the meal. And if you wanted dessert, you had better speak up or it was gone!

My parents are both gone, but they left a huge impact in this world through the legacy of their children and grandchildren. Even though my sisters and brothers are all scattered across the country, we are all very close. Some joined other family members and sought the sunshine of California (Rhonda, Eleanor), some embarked on the opportunities in the Southeast (Byron, Keith, Donna), and some remained to continue the traditions in the South (Gerald, Jennifer, Denise, Rene, Kenneth, Eric, Alvarez), and I settled in the Midwest. This large family has so many stories, so many wonderful memories, happy and tragic, but too many to recount. Every one is unique with their own blend of talents and gifts. Some are talented craftsmen, business experts, writers, civic leaders, and so on. But the common thread we all share is unconditional love, human compassion, neverending dedication to each other, and parents who inspired us all to be great human beings. This was the rare gift we received from our wonderful parents.

As in most New Orleans families, everything in our house revolved around food. Great food is something you savor and share with family and friends. When you enter a New Orleans home, the first thing you will be asked is "What can I get you to eat?" and you just can't refuse. Great food and entertaining is a unique experience you will always remember, especially in New Orleans, the "city that care forgot," because when you taste the food, all your troubles drift away. New Orleans is that rare combination of old traditions mixed with the anticipation of new and exciting experiences. The French influence is evident in the preparation of so many dishes and—like a good roux, the basis of any sauce in New Orleans cooking—is at the core of this great food. As I think back to the beginning of my passion for cooking, it is clear to me that it is rooted in the legacy of my mother, grandmother, and others who have influenced my love for cooking and entertaining. In memory and honor of my family, I bring these great recipes to all of you. I hope you enjoy them as much as I do.

Laissez les Bon Temps Rouler

Appetizers & Side Dishes

2 lbs. shrimp
8 quarts water
5 tablespoons Tony Chachere's Creole seasoning
½ cup finely chopped onions
½ cup finely chopped celery
1 cup mayonnaise
1 teaspoon ground black pepper

Using a 10-quart pot, boil shrimp in water and 2 tablespoons Creole seasoning for about 20 minutes, or until shrimp turn pink. Let cool for 30 minutes and peel. Chop shrimp and place in medium bowl. Add onions and celery and stir mixture. Add mayonnaise, remaining Creole seasoning, and pepper. Stir mixture thoroughly. Place in refrigerator and chill for 2 hours. Serve with buttered crackers.

The first time I made this for my husband, it immediately became one of his favorites. I would often make this dish for parties or as an appetizer before dinner. It didn't take long for it to be devoured. I think the combination of seafood and seasoning, along with the buttery crackers, was too much to resist. One spring when my sister El and brother-in-law David came to visit, he tasted this for the first time and was hooked! The dip was eaten so fast, I had to make another batch before the party started. Now this dip has become our family tradition to serve during the Saints football games.

Shrimp Dip

Cherry Tomatoes Stuffed with Tuna

2 lbs. cherry tomatoes
2 (6 oz.) packets or 2 cans of tuna in spring water
4 eggs, hard boiled and chopped
½ cup finely chopped onions
½ cup finely chopped celery
1 tablespoon finely chopped flat-leaf parsley
1 cup mayonnaise
1 tablespoon ground black pepper
1 tablespoon salt

Using a paring knife, cut off top of tomato and remove the inside. Set aside. Mix tuna, eggs, onions, celery, parsley, mayonnaise, salt, and pepper. Stuff tomatoes with tuna mixture.

Serves 15 to 20

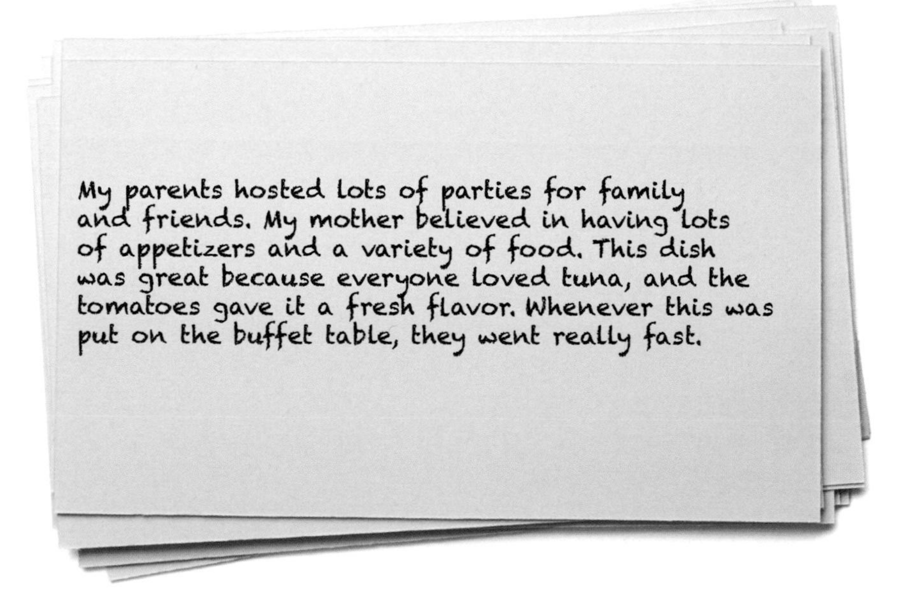

Rosemary Potatoes

2 lbs. russet potatoes, sliced
2 tablespoons salt
2 tablespoons ground black pepper
½ stick butter
¼ cup extra-virgin olive oil
½ cup finely chopped fresh rosemary

With the skin on, slice potatoes about ¼ inch thick and place in a 6 x 9-inch deep casserole dish. Season with salt and pepper. Melt butter and add olive oil. Pour mixture over potatoes and sprinkle with rosemary. Cover potatoes with aluminum foil and bake in a 400 degree oven for 20 minutes. Remove foil and continue to bake for 10 to 15 minutes, or until potatoes are tender.

Serves 6 to 8

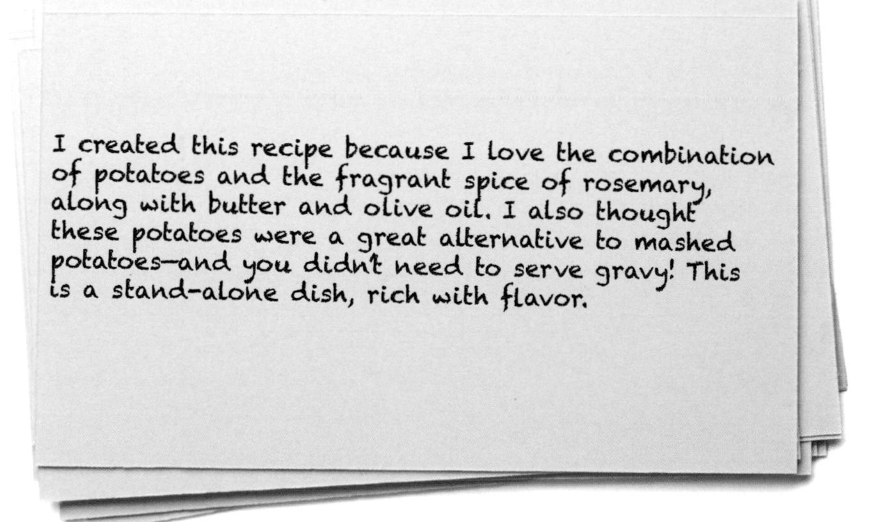
I created this recipe because I love the combination of potatoes and the fragrant spice of rosemary, along with butter and olive oil. I also thought these potatoes were a great alternative to mashed potatoes—and you didn't need to serve gravy! This is a stand-alone dish, rich with flavor.

Lyonnaise Potatoes

2 lbs. russet potatoes
2 medium onions, sliced
1 stick butter
2 tablespoons salt
2 tablespoons ground black pepper

Peel potatoes and slice about ½ inch thick. Set aside. Using a 12-inch skillet on medium/high heat, sauté onions in butter for about 10 minutes or until onions are soft. Add potatoes, salt and pepper, and stir mixture. Cover, reduce heat to medium/low, and cook for about 20 to 30 minutes, stirring constantly.

Serves 4 to 6

Most New Orleans dishes were served with rice, so when my mother did make potatoes, they were always well-received. Lyonnaise potatoes were a favorite because the combination of onions and butter made them tender and flavorful. With all the kids in the house, my father would buy a large sack of potatoes; it was the most economical way to buy them. The biggest job was peeling and cutting all those potatoes for dinner. My father said it was just like being in the army.

Lyonnaise Potatoes

New Orleans Potato Salad

2 lbs. russet potatoes
6 hard boiled eggs
1 tablespoon salt
1 tablespoon ground black pepper
½ cup chopped onions
½ cup chopped celery
1 tablespoon chopped fresh flat-leaf parsley
¼ cup chopped dill pickles
1 cup mayonnaise
2 tablespoons yellow mustard

Boil potatoes in water (with skin on) for about 30 to 45 minutes, or until potatoes are medium to soft. Using a large bowl, peel and cut potatoes in ¼ inch cubes. Cut boiled eggs into ½-inch cubes and place in bowl with potatoes. Add salt and pepper and toss together gently. Add onions, celery, parsley, and pickles. Thoroughly combine ingredients. Add mayonnaise and mustard and mix well. Serve warm immediately or refrigerate.

Serves 6 to 8

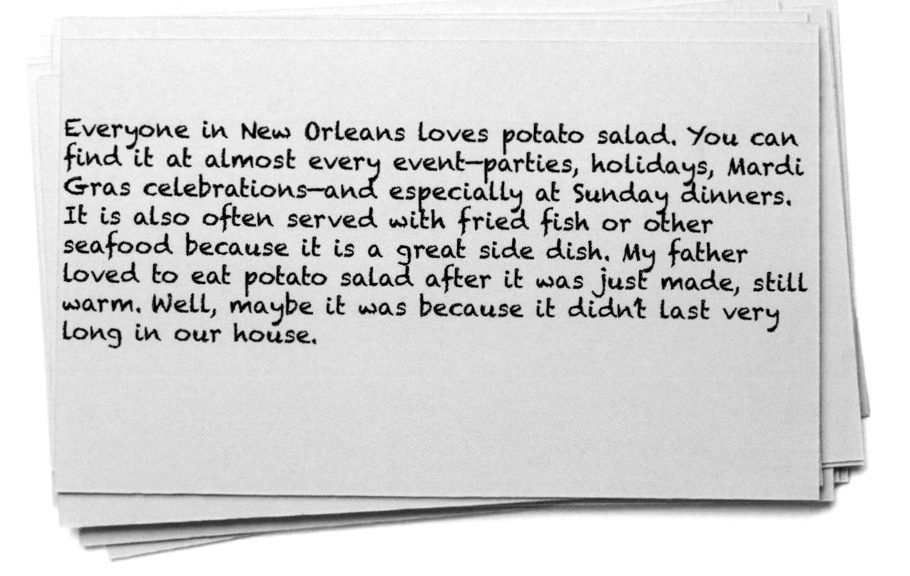

New Orleans Potato Salad

French Green Beans with Ham & Potatoes

2 strips bacon (cut in small slices)
¼ lb. ham (cut in small cubes)
1 tablespoon plain flour
1 lb. french-cut green beans
1 large potato (cut in small 1-inch cubes)
1 tablespoon salt
1 tablespoon ground black pepper
1 cup water

Using an 8-inch pot on medium heat, sauté bacon until crispy (about 5 to 10 minutes). Add cubed ham and cook for about 8 to 10 minutes. Add flour and stir well; cook for an additional 5 minutes. Add green beans, potatoes, salt and pepper, and stir well. Add water and cover. Reduce heat to medium and cook for about 15 to 20 minutes or until potatoes are soft.

Serves 4 to 6

This is a traditional French dish, referred to as "haricots verts" and prepared often in New Orleans. My mother always added the potatoes because it gave the dish more substance for feeding so many people. When she prepared these green beans, she used a very large pot because we all loved green beans. My mother used canned french-style green beans; I use fresh green beans, but I still use the french-style cut.

Stuffed Mushrooms

2 lbs. shiitake mushrooms, cleaned and cored
½ stick butter
⅓ cup finely chopped onions
⅓ cup finely chopped green peppers
¼ cup finely chopped celery
1 teaspoon finely chopped garlic
1 lb. fresh claw crabmeat
2 teaspoons Tony Chachere's Creole seasoning
1 teaspoon ground black pepper
¾ cup Italian bread crumbs (save ¼ cup for garnishing)

Place cleaned and cored mushrooms in a 9 x 9 casserole dish and put aside.

Crabmeat stuffing:

Using a 9-inch sauce pan, sauté onions, green peppers, celery, and garlic in butter for about 5 to 10 minutes, or until mixture is soft. Add crabmeat, Creole seasoning, and pepper. Cook about 5 minutes. Add bread crumbs and cook 10 to 12 minutes; mixture will thicken. Stuff crabmeat mixture in mushroom and sprinkle with remaining bread crumbs. Bake at 350 degrees for 10 to 15 minutes.

Serves 6 to 8

My husband loves mushrooms, and while they are not my favorite, I do make these for him. As it turned out, they became an instant hit at parties. or as an appetizer before a holiday meal. I think the secret is using fresh crabmeat and the little button mushrooms—the kind you could just pop right into your mouth. While this is not typically a New Orleans dish, I have also learned to enjoy them.

Homemade Biscuits

2 cups all-purpose flour
1 tablespoon baking powder
2 tablespoons granulated sugar
1 teaspoon salt
1 stick cold butter, diced
1 cup whole milk

In a large bowl, mix flour, baking powder, sugar, and salt. Using a fork, cut butter into flour mix until completely incorporated; there will be small pieces of butter. Add milk and stir until fully mixed. Gently roll out dough into a floured board into 1-inch thickness. Using a small biscuit cutter, cut biscuits and place on a cookie sheet. Bake at 450 degrees for 12 to 15 minutes.

Makes 12 to 15 biscuits

We were a family that loved biscuits, and my brothers loved when I made them. I think it's because in New Orleans everyone drank coffee (chicory coffee), and we loved flaky, buttery biscuits served with coffee, especially to dunk. Biscuits were versatile; you could serve them at any meal. My father would put scrambled eggs on his biscuits for breakfast, or pile one high with ham for lunch. Of course, we also loved to slather those biscuits with butter and jam, right out of the oven; they disappeared fast.

Main Dishes

New Orleans Creole Gumbo

4 quarts water
4 quarts chicken stock or seafood stock
½ cup vegetable oil
1 lb. ham, cut up in cubes
1 lb. beef smoked sausage, sliced
1 lb. hot sausage or andouille sausage
1 lb. boneless, skinless chicken breast (cut up in cubes) seasoned with salt and pepper
4 chicken wings, seasoned with salt and pepper
1 turkey wing, seasoned with salt and pepper
1 cup chopped onions
1 cup chopped green peppers
1 cup chopped green onions
3 cloves of garlic, finely chopped
¼ cup finely chopped flat-leaf parsley
3 tablespoons ground black pepper
2 tablespoons Tony Chachere's Creole seasoning
1 teaspoon thyme
2 tablespoons gumbo filé
3 tablespoons salt
4 large bay leaves
2 lbs. shrimp (peeled and deveined) seasoned with salt and pepper
1 cup small oysters (optional)
2 blue crabs, cleaned and split in half (optional)
White rice, cooked

Place water and stock in 10-quart pot on medium heat, cook for about ½ hour or until liquid is warm. Add ¼ cup of oil to 11-inch skillet and heat at medium to high until hot. Separately, sauté ham, sausages, chicken, and turkey (about 5 to 10 minutes or until partially cooked), then place each ingredient in stock pot. Using the same skillet, pour remaining oil into pan. Add onions, green peppers, green onions, garlic, and parsley and cook until mixture is soft (about 10 minutes); add to stock pot. Add roux then stir, completely incorporating roux into liquid. Add black pepper, Creole seasoning, thyme, filé, salt, and bay leaves and stir mixture well. Cover, reduce heat to medium/low, and cook for about 2 hours (stirring occasionally). Meat will start to become tender and gumbo will thicken. Using a spoon, skim excess grease off the top of the gumbo and discard. Add shrimp, oysters, and crabs. Stir mixture and cook for 1 more hour. Serve in bowls over white rice.

Serves 12 to 15 people

Making the Roux:

1 stick unsalted butter
½ cup vegetable oil
1½ cups plain flour

Add oil and butter to an 11-inch skillet. On high, heat for about 5 minutes or until mixture is hot. Reduce heat to medium and add flour. Using a whisk, stir until mixture is completely incorporated. Stir constantly to prevent burning until mixture starts to darken to a mahogany color (about 10 to 15 minutes). If mixture burns, discard and start over. Burnt roux will negatively affect the outcome of any dish.

*For best results, use a cast-iron skillet.

When I was growing up, gumbo was a big deal—we all LOVED it! My mother didn't cook it too often (it was very expensive and it took an entire day to cook in that large pot). When my mother did make gumbo, it was fabulous and everyone came from miles away to sit at the table with a steaming bowl; it was everyone's favorite. Gumbo was cooked in a pot so big it barely fit on the stove, but you could smell the aroma and those wonderful spices all through the house. Of course, with all the family and friends who ate her gumbo, there were never any leftovers – never! At the end of the evening you were scraping the pot just to get a piece of sausage. Good luck next time!

New Orleans Creole Gumbo

Jambalaya

Jambalaya

½ pound beef smoked sausage (cut into cubes)
½ pound ham (cut into cubes)
½ pound boneless, skinless chicken breast (cut into cubes)
¼ cup olive oil
1 cup chopped onion
1 cup chopped green pepper
¼ cup chopped garlic
2 pounds raw shrimp (peeled and deveined)
1½ cups uncooked long grain white rice*
1 cup tomato sauce
1 cup chicken broth
1 tablespoon ground black pepper
2 tablespoons Tony Chachere's Creole seasoning
3 large bay leaves
¼ cup chopped flat-leaf parsley
Pinch of salt

*To avoid stickiness, rinse rice grains in cool water before cooking.

Using an 11-inch skillet on medium heat, sauté sausage, ham, and chicken in olive oil for about 10 minutes (just until the meat is lightly cooked on the outside). Add onions, green peppers, and garlic and cook, stirring frequently until they are soft (about 10 minutes). Add shrimp and cook until shrimp are lightly pink on both sides (about 10-15 minutes). Add rice, tomato sauce, chicken broth, and mix well. Add black pepper, Creole seasoning, bay leaves, and parsley. Also add a pinch of salt, but you don't need a lot since Creole seasoning contains salt. Turn temperature to low. Cover and let cook for about 15 minutes. The rice should start to absorb the liquid; if it looks too dry, add more chicken broth. Cook until the rice is tender (about another 20-25 minutes). Turn off heat and let stand for about 15 minutes.

Serves 6 to 8

Jambalaya's Story

There are so many variations of this dish throughout Louisiana, and also across the country. It is the mixture of flavors—saugage, shrimp, chicken, or whatever you like that makes it so special. My mother would make Jambalaya when she had leftover ham from Sunday dinner (which was rare) or my father bought home extra sausage from the store. It was one of those dishes that you could just combine everything in one pot (which made washing dishes easy for me and my sisters), but always a New Orleans classic.

1 cup chopped onions
1 cup chopped green pepper
½ cup chopped celery
3 large cloves of garlic, finely chopped
¼ cup vegetable oil
1 cup chicken broth
2 tablespoons Tony Chachere's Creole seasoning
1 tablespoon ground black pepper
3 large bay leaves
1 lb. cooked crawfish tails

Using a deep 12-inch skillet, sauté onions, green pepper, celery, and garlic in oil until soft (about 5 to 10 minutes). Add roux and stir well, incorporating all ingredients. Add chicken broth, stir well, and then add Creole seasoning, black pepper, and bay leaves. Reduce heat to medium, cover and cook for about 30 minutes. Add crawfish tails and stir well. Cover and let cook for about 30 to 45 minutes. Serve over white rice.

Serves 6 to 10

Making the Roux:

½ cup vegetable oil
¾ cup plain flour
2 cups chicken stock (or crawfish stock)

Add oil to an 11-inch skillet.* On high, heat oil for about 5 minutes or until the mixture is hot. Reduce heat to medium and add flour. Using a whisk, stir until mixture is completely incorporated. Stir constantly to prevent burning until mixture starts to darken to a peanut-butter color (about 10 to 15 minutes). If mixture burns, discard and start over. Burnt roux will negatively affect the outcome of any dish.

* For best results, use a cast-iron skillet.

Crawfish Etoufee's Story

Mud bugs are what I often heard to describe crawfish. Most people just can't get over how they look. I call them "mini-lobster," but they actually have a taste all their own. Crawfish was considered the cheap man's lobster, and during the spring and summer in New Orleans, they were plentiful. Crawfish boils are a common practice during the summer in New Orleans and everyone has a big pot for cooking them. Loading the pot with crawfish, potatoes, and mini-corn-on-the-cobs, and the main ingredient–seafood boil. The aroma is so intense that you have to walk away from the pot so you don't inhale the fumes too fast. This dish was always a special treat because, so many times, we ate all the boiled crawfish before my mother could save enough to make etoufee.

Crawfish Etoufee

Seafood Pie

Shrimp & Crabmeat Pie (Seafood Pie)

½ cup chopped onion
½ cup chopped green pepper
3 cloves of garlic, finely chopped
¾ stick butter
1 lb. shrimp (peeled, deveined, and chopped)
1 lb. fresh claw crabmeat
1 (10 oz.) can cream of mushroom soup
1 cup grated mild cheddar cheese (save ¼ cup for topping)
½ cup Italian bread crumbs
1 teaspoon ground black pepper
1 tablespoon Tony Chachere's Creole seasoning
¼ teaspoon Lea & Perrins Worcestershire sauce
1 unbaked 9-inch pie crust

On medium heat, sauté onions, green peppers, and garlic in butter for about 10 minutes or until mixture is soft. Add shrimp and sauté 10-12 minutes or until shrimp are pink. Add crabmeat and cook another 5 minutes. Add cream of mushroom soup and cook for 5-8 minutes. Add cheese and cook another 5 minutes. Add bread crumbs, pepper, Creole seasoning, and Worcestershire sauce. Cook for 8-10 minutes (mixture will become thick). Pour mixture into pie crust and top with remaining cheddar cheese. Bake at 350 degrees for 15-20 minutes.

Serves 8 to 10

Shrimp & Crabmeat Pie's Story

My sisters and I each have our own variation of this recipe, but my sister Rhonda added new ingredients. We created this recipe because we just loved all the ingredients and thought the combination was an experience in seafood heaven. But let it be said, this is my husband's favorite taste of New Orleans. For years my daughters didn't like this, and he was fine with that. When they got older, they embraced the delightful combination of ingredients, just as he did. I have made this dish countless times, and each time my husband—serving as my taster—would proclaim "This is the best you have ever made." Thanks for the encouragement and your expert taste buds.

Red Beans & Rice

5 quarts water
2 lbs. Camellia red kidney beans
¼ cup vegetable oil
1 lb. ham cut in cubes
1 lb. beef smoked sausage cut in cubes
1 cup chopped onions
½ cup chopped green pepper
⅓ cup plain flour
3 tablespoons salt
3 tablespoons ground black pepper
1 teaspoon thyme
3 large bay leaves
White rice, cooked

Using an 8-quart pot, soak red beans in water for about 1 hour. Beans will become wrinkled and absorb some of the water. Place pot on medium heat, cover and cook for about 1½ hours, stirring occasionally. Using a 10-inch skillet, heat oil in pan on medium heat. Sauté ham and sausage in oil for about 10 minutes, or until mixture is slightly brown around the edges. Remove and place on paper towel to drain, then add to beans. Using the same skillet, sauté onions and green pepper for about 5 to 10 minutes, or until mixture is slightly soft. Add flour and cook another 5 minutes, stirring constantly. Place mixture in beans and stir. Add salt, pepper, thyme, and bay leaves. Cover and simmer on medium/low heat for about 2½ to 3 hours (stirring occasionally), or until beans start to thicken and become soft. Serve over white rice.

Serves 6-8

Red Beans and Rice's Story

The story goes that every Monday in New Orleans was laundry day; this dates back to the 1800s. You could put on a pot of beans and they could cook all day, giving you time to get your laundry done. Just about every restaurant (from the smallest to the finest) and household in New Orleans serves red beans and rice on Mondays. But the result is pure delight. My mother also engaged in this ritual, but the truth is, she did laundry every single day. Red beans and rice was one of her specialties. She would soak her beans overnight and they would promptly go on the stove early in the morning. Of course, she had to make three pounds of beans, along with cooking four cups of rice (well, sometimes she would burn the rice). We all loved when Mondays rolled around because it meant the taste of tender beans cooked with meats, served over fluffy white rice.

Red Beans & Rice

Stuffed Bell Peppers

3 medium green peppers (cut in half, seeds removed) to stuff
2 lbs. lean ground beef
½ lb. ham, cut up into small cubes
½ lb. shrimp (peeled & deveined), cut up in small pieces
1 cup chopped onions
1 cup chopped green peppers
¾ cup Italian bread crumbs (save ¼ cup for garnishing)
¼ cup water
1 teaspoon salt
3 tablespoons ground black pepper
1 teaspoon thyme

Boil green peppers in water (covering them with water completely) for about 30 minutes or until peppers are soft. Set aside.

Using a 9-inch sauce pan, sauté ground beef until brown (about 15-20 minutes). Remove excess grease from pan and discard. Add ham and cook about 5 minutes, then add shrimp and cook another 10 minutes (or until shrimp are pink). Add onions and green peppers and cook for about 5 to 8 minutes (or until onions and green peppers are soft). Combine ½ cup bread crumbs with ¼ cup water and set aside. Add salt, pepper, thyme, and bread crumbs mixture and cook for 10 minutes (mixture will become thick).

Stuff mixture in peppers then sprinkle with remaining ¼ cup bread crumbs. Bake at 350 degrees for 10 to 15 minutes.

Serves 6

Stuffed Bell Peppers' Story

This is a classic New Orleans Creole dish. There are lots of variations of stuffed bell peppers, but leave it to New Orleans to add shrimp every chance they can get. With so many people to feed, my mother would buy out the vegetable truck when it came around so she would have enough green peppers to make this dish. My sisters and I had to carefully slice the peppers in half without breaking them, because if we did, that meant one less pepper for dinner. I think the unique combination of ground beef, ham, and shrimp makes the peppers so flavorful.

Oyster Dressing

1 lb. lean ground beef
1 lb. oysters, chopped
½ cup chopped onions
½ cup chopped green pepper
1 teaspoon salt
2 tablespoons ground black pepper
1 teaspoon thyme
½ cup Italian bread crumbs (save ¼ cup for garnishing)

In a 9-inch sauce pan, sauté ground beef until browned (about 15 minutes). Remove excess grease from pan and discard. Add oysters and cook about 10 minutes. Mixture may be a little watery. Add onions and green peppers and cook for 5 minutes or until mixture is soft. Add salt, pepper, thyme, and ¼ cup of bread crumbs. Cook for another 15 minutes or until mixture is fully incorporated and thickens. Place in a 9-inch casserole dish and sprinkle with remaining bread crumbs. Bake at 350 degrees for 15 to 20 minutes.

Serves 6 to 8

* For oyster patties, place mixture in mini pastry shells.

Everyone in New Orleans knows that you only eat oysters in the months with an 'R'—beginning with September and ending with April. During these months, the cool waters of the Gulf of Mexico and Lake Pontchartrain make the oysters prime for harvesting. It is also said that during the summer months when the oysters reproduce, they don't possess their natural sweet flavors (the water is too warm). Whatever the reason, we never had oysters during the summer. When my father did get oysters, he would bring home a sack (probably around 20 pounds) of oysters. He would set up an assembly line operation where he would grab the oyster, and using his special "oyster knife," shuck them and either leave them on the half-shell for devouring, or toss them in a big bowl. My mother would fry them or use them for oyster dressing. During our traditional Thanksgiving dinner, we always had oyster dressing with our turkey.

Stewed Chicken (Coq au vin)

¼ cup vegetable oil
3 lbs. chicken (bone-in), cut up and seasoned with salt and pepper
1 cup chopped onions
1 cup chopped celery
2 tablespoons plain flour
1 can chicken broth
½ cup dry white wine
1 teaspoon salt
2 tablespoons ground black pepper
1 teaspoon thyme
2 bay leaves
2 cups white rice, cooked

Using a deep 12-inch pot, sauté chicken in vegetable oil for about 10 to 15 minutes or until chicken is semi-cooked and slightly brown around the edges. Remove and place on paper towel to drain. Add onions and celery, and cook until mixture is soft (about 5 minutes). Add flour and cook about 5 minutes, or until mixture is fully incorporated. Add chicken broth and wine, and cook for about 10 minutes. Add salt, pepper, bay leaves, and thyme. Cover and let entire mixture cook on low heat about 30 minutes. Add chicken, stir mixture completely and cover. Put on low heat and cook for about 1 hour. Serve over white rice.

Serves 6 to 8

My mother was very proud of her French heritage and this dish was a classic. While the actual dish is called Coq au vin, this is my mother's version. Of course we all loved when she would fry chicken, but this dish was usually made when she was busy sewing and she could leave the chicken on the stove to simmer for hours. The smell of the chicken cooking made you feel like you were sitting at a French cafe surrounded by the sights and sounds of the City of Light. The chicken was so tender it just fell right off the bone, and with a biscuit or French bread, you could sop up the wonderful sauce.

New Orleans Dirty Rice

New Orleans Dirty Rice

2 lbs. lean ground beef
1 cup chopped onions
1 cup chopped green pepper
½ cup chopped celery
1 tablespoon salt
3 tablespoons ground black pepper
2 cups cooked white rice

Using an 11-inch skillet, cook ground beef for about 15 to 20 minutes, making sure you separate chunks. Remove excess grease. Add onions, green peppers, celery, salt, and pepper. Cook for 10 to 15 minutes. Remove from heat and let cool for about 10 minutes. Fold cooked white rice into mixture, incorporating all ingredients.

Serves 10 to 12

This is one of those dishes that is great when you have a large group. My sister Denise was our resident expert at making dirty rice. We made this often when we would have large, extended family dinners or parties, or it was a great dish to serve when you hosted a Mardi Gras event. I think it tastes wonderful even cold. Lots of New Orleans families prepare their version of Dirty Rice and it is very popular at any event.

½ stick butter
⅓ cup finely chopped onions
⅓ cup finely chopped green peppers
¼ cup finely chopped celery
1 teaspoon finely chopped garlic
1 lb. fresh jumbo lump crabmeat
2 teaspoons Tony Chachere's Creole seasoning
1 teaspoon ground black pepper
¾ cup Italian bread crumbs (save ¼ cup for garnishing)

Using a 9-inch sauce pan, sauté onions, green peppers, celery, and garlic in butter for about 5 to 10 minutes, or until mixture is soft. Add crabmeat, Creole seasoning, and pepper, and cook for about 5 minutes. Add ½ cup Italian bread crumbs and cook 10 to 12 minutes (mixture will thicken). Place in an 8-inch casserole pan and sprinkle with remaining ¼ cup bread crumbs. Bake at 350 degrees for 10 to 15 minutes.

Serves 6 to 8

Crabmeat is one of those delicacies that is so versatile to cook with, plus you could eat it anytime of the day or night, even cold. Fresh crabmeat was plentiful and was always available when I was growing up. I loved to eat it right out of the container. When my mother would make this dish, she would stuff the crabmeat in the little tin foil molds shaped like crabs. She would make about three dozen stuffed crabs for just one meal.

2 lbs. catfish, thinly sliced (salt and pepper to season)
2 eggs, lightly beaten
½ cup whole milk
2 cups yellow cornmeal
2 tablespoons plain flour
1 cup vegetable oil

Season both sides of fish with salt and pepper, set aside. In medium bowl, combine eggs and milk, and beat slightly. Place cornmeal and flour in separate medium bowl and combine. Dip fish in egg/milk mixture then dredge fish in cornmeal/flour mixture. Shake off excess.

Using a 12-inch skillet (for best results use cast-iron skillet), heat oil in skillet on medium/high heat. Place fish into hot oil. Do not overcrowd pan. Fry on both sides until golden brown (about 3 or 4 minutes per side). Remove fish, place on paper towel.

Serves 4 to 6

My father loved to fish and would come home with the fresh fish of the day. While most of the time it would be trout, there were some occasions when he would come home with catfish. Catfish, he said, were the "scum of the sea." With their cat-like whiskers and dark, scaly exterior, catfish were not widely the fish of choice in New Orleans. My family loved them because they had a strong, bold flavor. They lived at the bottom of the sea, but were very tasty.

Shrimp Creole

1/3 cup vegetable oil
1 cup chopped onion
1 cup chopped green pepper
1 cup chopped celery
1 tablespoon finely chopped garlic
1/4 cup plain flour
2 (15 oz. cans) tomato sauce (4 cups)
1/3 cup water (or seafood stock or chicken stock)*
2 large bay leaves
2 tablespoons Tony Chachere's Creole seasoning
1 teaspoon ground black pepper
1/2 teaspoon thyme
2 lbs. shrimp (peeled and deveined)
(Season raw shrimp with salt and pepper)
2 cups cooked white rice
4 stalks chopped green onions (for finishing)

Using a 12-inch skillet, sauté onions, green peppers, celery, and garlic in vegetable oil on medium-high heat for about 10-12 minutes (mixture should be soft and wilted). Add flour and stir frequently for about 5 minutes, until flour is fully incorporated. Add tomato sauce, water, bay leaves, Creole seasoning, pepper, and thyme. Stir until mixture is fully incorporated. Cover and simmer on medium-low heat for about 30 minutes; stir occasionally to make sure nothing sticks. Season shrimp with salt and pepper. Add shrimp to mixture, cover, and cook for another 15-20 minutes. Serve over white rice, and garnish with green onions.

Serves 4-6

* To make seafood stock: After peeling shrimp, boil shells in a pot of 2 cups of water for about 15-20 minutes.

Shrimp Creole's Story

Growing up in New Orleans, there were always entrepreneurs around willing to sell you something. Since seafood was plentiful, we could count on a guy in a truck riding through the neighborhood with a cooler full of fresh shrimp. When he would pull up in front of our house, my mother would carefully inspect the catch, then order ten pounds of shrimp. The driver would reach in his truck, promptly pull out a scale to weigh the order, wrap the shrimp in newspaper, count his cash, then he was on his way. My sisters and I then had the task of peeling and deveining all those shrimp until it felt like our fingers were raw, but it was worth the effort. This was also the first New Orleans dish I ever made for my husband. I think it started him on the path to a love affair with me and New Orleans food.

Sautéed Trout with Lemon and Butter (Trout Meuniere)

Salt and pepper to season
1 large rainbow trout (cut in half, deboned, and filleted)
1 cup plain flour
1 stick butter
1 tablespoon fresh lemon juice
Pinch of lemon zest
1 tablespoon chopped shallots
1 teaspoon of flat-leaf parsley, chopped

Season fish with salt and pepper on both sides, then dredge in flour. Using a large pan, melt ½ stick of butter. Add fish and cook for 5 to 10 minutes, or until the edge of the fish looks crisp. Turn over and cook the other side 5 to 10 minutes. You should only flip once. Remove and set aside. Add remaining butter, lemon juice, zest, and shallots to pan. Cook about 2 minutes (sauce will look slightly thick). Pour sauce over fish. Garnish with parsley.

Serves 4

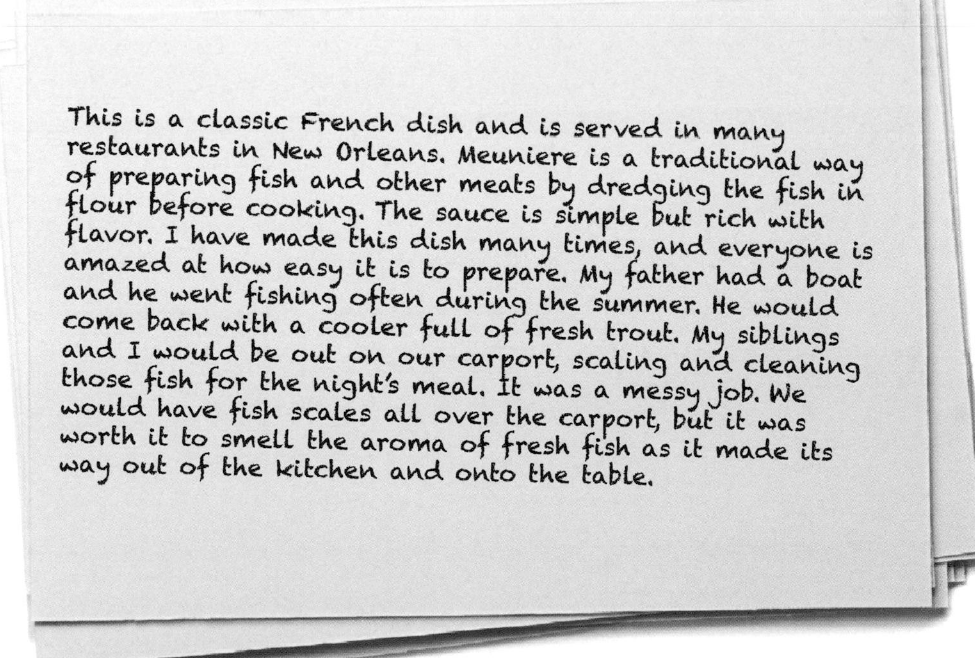

Stuffed Shrimp Soldiers

2 lbs. large shrimp (peeled and deveined), keeping tail fin
Salt and pepper shrimp to season
1/3 cup finely chopped onions
1/3 cup finely chopped green peppers
1/4 cup finely chopped celery
1 teaspoon finely chopped garlic
1 stick butter
1 lb. fresh jumbo lump crabmeat
2 teaspoons Tony Chachere's Creole seasoning
1 teaspoon ground black pepper
1/2 cup Italian bread crumbs

Using a paring knife, slit shrimp along the back to the tail fin. Be sure not to cut through the shrimp. Season shrimp with salt and pepper. Place shrimp on cookie sheet with the bottom down and tail fin curled up over shrimp. Using a 9-inch sauce pan, sauté onions, green peppers, celery, and garlic in 1/2 stick butter for about 5 to 10 minutes or until mixture is soft. Add crabmeat, Creole seasoning, and pepper, and cook about 5 minutes. Add bread crumbs and cook 10 to 12 minutes (mixture will thicken). Let cool for about 20 minutes. Stuff each shrimp with about 1 tablespoon of crabmeat mixture. Bake at 350 degrees for 15 to 20 minutes, occasionally basting with remaining melted butter.

Serves 4 to 6

Stuffed Shrimp's Story

This is one of my favorite dishes. I love the combination of shrimp and fresh crabmeat, and the presentation is so appealing. This was something that I created based on my love of the combination of shrimp and crab. Whenever I make this for dinner or parties, everyone just can't get enough of them.

Roasted Pork Tenderloin

2 lbs. pork tenderloin
6 gloves of garlic, cut in quarters
2 tablespoons salt
2 tablespoons ground black pepper
½ cup chopped onions
¾ cup chicken stock
¼ cup of plain flour

Using a sharp knife, gently poke a ½-inch slit throughout the roast (about 5 slits on each side of the meat). Then stuff a piece of garlic in each hole, making sure it goes all the way down in the roast. Generously season the rib roast on each side with salt and pepper. Place roast in a deep, 8 x12 roasting pan. Sprinkle ½ cup of onions on top of roast, and add ½ cup chicken stock to base of pan (save ¼ cup for sauce). Cover and place in preheated oven at 350 degrees. Cook for 2 to 2½ hours.

Sauce:

Remove roast from pan. Place pan on medium heat and bring juices to boil. Add flour and whisk until flour is incorporated in sauce (about 10 minutes). Whisk in chicken stock, reduce heat, and cook another 10 minutes. Slice roast and place in sauce.

Serves 6 to 8

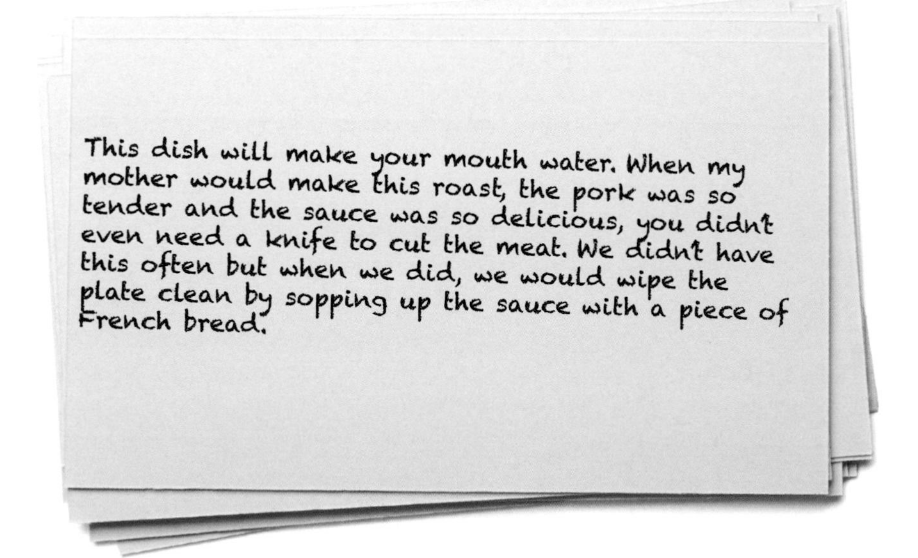

Crawfish Pasta

½ cup finely chopped shallots
¼ cup finely chopped garlic
1 stick butter, unsalted
1 lb. crawfish tails, cooked
1 (15 oz.) jar Bertolli Alfredo Sauce
1 tablespoon ground black pepper
2 tablespoons Tony Chachere's Creole seasoning
½ lb. angel-hair pasta, cooked

Using an 11-inch skillet, sauté shallots and garlic in butter for about 5 minutes, or until mixture is soft. Add crawfish, cover and cook for 10 to 15 minutes. Add Alfredo sauce, pepper, and Creole seasoning. Cover and cook for 10 to 15 minutes, stirring occasionally. Serve over angel-hair pasta.

Serves 6 to 8

Crawfish season is typically during the warm spring and summer months. My sister Jennifer loves to make this dish. When I was growing up, my father would bring home a sack of crawfish, still alive. I remember seeing those "mud bugs," as we used to call them, moving around in the sack desperately trying to escape. When he would open the sack, they just started fighting for their lives. My brothers would grab a crawfish or two and hold it up to my face just to hear me scream. But when my father put the crawfish in that large pot, along with mini-corn, petite potatoes, and seafood boil, we all waited happily for the delicious results. I began making this dish because of my love for crawfish and to celebrate the season of "mud bugs."

Crawfish Pasta

Creole Style Rib Roast

Creole Style Rib Roast

1 rib roast, 8–10 lb., bone-in
8 cloves garlic, cut in halves
2 tablespoons salt
2 tablespoons ground black pepper
1/3 cup finely chopped onions
1 tablespoon plain flour
3/4 cup water

Pre-heat oven to 350 degrees. Using a sharp knife, poke a 1-inch slit throughout the roast (about 5 slits on each side of the meat), then stuff a piece of garlic in each hole. Make sure it goes all the way down in the roast. Generously season the rib roast on each side with salt and pepper. Place rib roast in a deep 8 x 12 roasting pan. Sprinkle onions on top of roast, then flour. Add water to base of pan. Cover and place in pre-heated oven. Cook for 1½ hours, then turn roast over. Cover and cook for another 1½ hours.

Serves 6 to 8

When I was growing up, we rarely had roast beef. There was so much fresh seafood available—and it was certainly a lot less expensive. When my mother did make roast, this was a family favorite. Of course, every New Orleans cook loves garlic, and she was no exception. My mother said stuffing the roast with garlic would season the inside of the meat and she would rub salt and pepper over the entire roast for that deep, rich flavor. When the roast was cooking, you could smell that garlic all over the house. Not only was it good for your heart, she said, it also kept the vampires away.

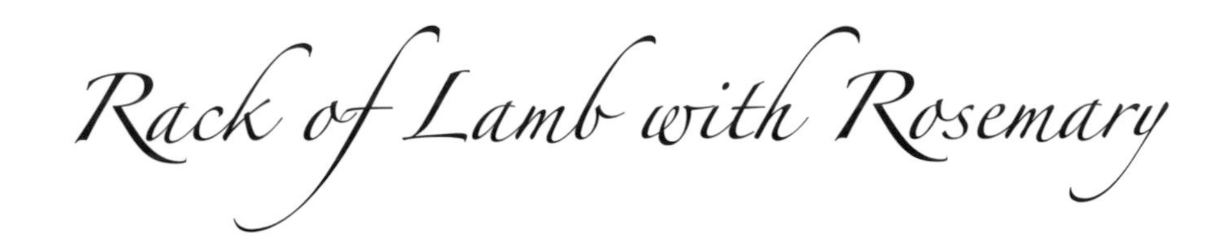

Rack of Lamb with Rosemary

2 racks of "frenched" lamb*
1 tablespoon salt
1 tablespoon ground black pepper
Juice of 1 small lemon
½ cup finely chopped fresh rosemary
½ cup chicken stock

Generously season lamb racks with salt and pepper. Pour lemon juice on lamb and then sprinkle with fresh rosemary. Add chicken stock to base of pan. Cover and place in oven at 350 degrees for 2 hours.

* A frenched rack of lamb has the meat and fat cut away from the tips to expose the bone.

Serves 4 to 6

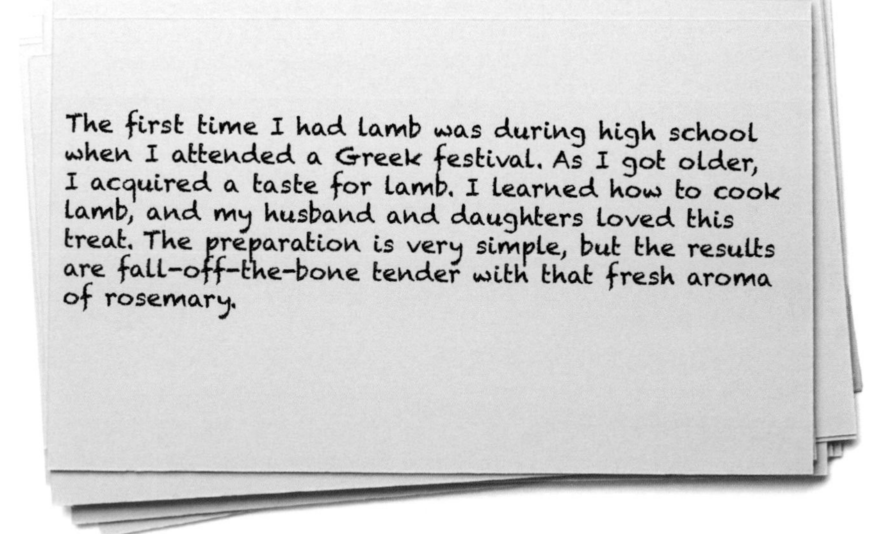

Stuffed Mirliton

10-12 mirliton
½ stick unsalted butter
1 cup chopped onions
1 tablespoon chopped garlic
2 lbs. shrimp (peeled and deveined), coarsely cut up
1 tablespoon salt
1 tablespoon ground black pepper
1 tablespoon Tony Chachere's Creole seasoning
2 cups Italian bread crumbs (plus 1 tablespoon for topping)

Using an 8-quart pot, boil mirliton in water for about 30 minutes, or until mirliton are soft and tender. Test by sticking them with a fork. Let cool and cut lengthwise. Using a large spoon, remove and discard seed. Scrape pulp from the shells and place in a large colander to drain excess water.

Using an 11-inch sauce pan on medium heat, sauté onions and garlic in butter for about 10 minutes or until mixture is soft. Add shrimp and cook about 10 minutes, until shrimp are pink. Add mirliton, salt, pepper, Creole seasoning, and stir mixture. Cook for about 10 to 15 minutes. Gradually add bread crumbs; this will thicken mixture. Stir constantly to prevent sticking. Pour mixture into a 9x11 casserole dish. Sprinkle with remaining bread crumbs. Bake at 350 degrees for 20 to 30 minutes.

Serves 6 to 8

New Orleans natives rarely ate traditional squash, but loved this variety. Lots of homes in New Orleans grew mirliton right in their backyards. The warm, humid weather made the squash grow like wildfire. In traditional New Orleans fashion, shrimp was added to this dish, which adds a unique dimension of flavor. My mother grew a mirliton vine in our yard. She got lots of satisfaction knowing that she could step out of the house and pick them fresh off the vine for dinner.

1 whole turkey, 10-lb.
3 tablespoons salt
3 tablespoons ground black pepper
1 stick butter, melted
¼ cup fresh rosemary, finely chopped
1 cup chicken stock

Generously season turkey with salt and pepper. To add depth of flavor, carefully season under skin of turkey breast. Place turkey into roasting pan. Melt butter and pour over turkey, making sure all parts of turkey are covered. Sprinkle rosemary over entire turkey. For added flavor, carefully separate the skin from the breast of the turkey and rub butter and rosemary as deep as you can between the skin and the meat. Be careful not to tear the skin of the turkey. Add chicken stock to base of turkey. Cover and cook at 350 degrees for 3 hours. Remove cover, baste turkey, and cook for another 15 to 20 minutes, or until turkey starts to brown on the outside. Remove from oven, cover and let rest for 30 minutes before carving.

For Turkey Gravy:

½ cup finely chopped onions
¼ cup vegetable oil
½ cup plain flour
2 cups turkey drippings
1 tablespoon ground black pepper

Using an 8-inch sauce pan, sauté onions in oil for about 5 minutes, or until onions are soft. Add flour and cook for another 10 minutes; stir constantly until mixture starts to brown. Add turkey drippings and pepper. Cover and cook for about 10 to 15 minutes; whisk occasionally. Gravy will start to thicken.

Roasted Turkey's Story

My husband is a "turkey junkie"—he just loves turkey and I cook it often throughout the year. But when it comes to a holiday, I make the best turkey and gravy in our family. Whenever I visit my sisters for Thanksgiving dinner, I am always asked to make the turkey. The secret to my delicious turkey is seasoning it with a generouse amount of salt and pepper (and butter), then cooking it slow and covered to keep in all the juices. The other important ingredient in my turkey is fresh rosemary, which brings out the natural falvor of turkey. My husband and daughters love the gravy so much, I catch them in the kitchen, spoon in hand, as my tasters because they just can't wait until dinner.

Chicken Fricassee (Creole Chicken)

3 pounds boneless, skinless chicken breast
(cut in 1-inch pieces and season with salt & pepper)
1/3 cup vegetable oil
1 cup chopped onion
1 tablespoon finely chopped garlic
1 cup chopped green pepper
1/4 cup plain flour
2 (15 oz. cans) tomato sauce (4 cups)
1/3 cup chicken stock
2 large bay leaves
2 teaspoons ground black pepper
1/2 teaspoon thyme
1 lb. cooked medium egg noodles

Using a 12-inch skillet, sauté chicken in vegetable oil on medium heat for about 15 minutes or until chicken is semi-cooked. Remove from pan and set aside. Add onions, garlic, and green peppers and cook for about 12-15 minutes (mixture should be soft and wilted). Add flour and stir until fully inforporated. Cook for about 5 minutes, stirring frequently. Add tomato sauce, chicken stock, bay leaves, pepper, and thyme. Stir until mixture is well-blended. Cover and simmer on medium-low heat for about 30 minutes, stirring occasionally to make sure nothing sticks. Add chicken, cover, and cook for another 15-20 minutes. Serve over medium egg noodles.

Serves 4 to 6

Chicken Fricassee's Story

So many families in New Orleans have their version of Chicken Fricassee, but this dish used to be referred to as "Creole Chicken." It started as an alternative to shrimp Creole, during those times when you didn't have shrimp, or if someone was allergic to seafood (heaven forbid). Since residents of New Orleans also love chicken, it became very popular with the locals. To add a different flavor, most people serve the chicken with noodles.

Smothered Pork Chops

4 thin-sliced center-cut pork chops
Salt and pepper to season pork chops
¼ cup vegetable oil
1 large onion, sliced
¼ cup plain flour
1 cup chicken stock
1 teaspoon salt
1 tablespoon black pepper

Generously season pork chops with salt and pepper. Using an 11-inch skillet, heat oil on medium/high heat. Place pork chops in skillet and cook for about 3 minutes on each side until golden brown. Remove chops and place on paper towel to drain. Add onions to skillet and sauté for about 5 minutes, stirring constantly until onions are soft. Add flour and cook another 8 to 10 minutes, stirring constantly. Mixture will start to turn brown. Add chicken stock, reduce heat to medium, cover, and simmer for about 15 minutes, stirring occasionally. Add salt and pepper. Add pork chops, making sure they are completely immersed in the sauce. Cover and cook on medium/low heat for 40 to 50 minutes. Serve over mashed potatoes.

Serves 2 to 4

This was one of my father's favorite meals; he loved pork chops. I think that's why I have such a fondness for this dish. When my mother seasoned the pork chops, she always added extra pepper; it really gave them a more spicy bite. She loved the thin-sliced pork chops, but I think she asked the butcher to cut them thin because she had so many people to feed. The peppery sauce was wonderful layered over light, fluffy mashed potatoes.

Smothered Pork Chops

Mother's Fried Chicken

1 large whole chicken (cut up in pieces)
Salt and pepper
2 cups plain flour
2 cups vegetable oil

Generously season chicken with salt and pepper. For best results, season chicken the night before. Place flour in large bowl. Using a 12-inch skillet (for best results, use a cast-iron skillet), heat oil to 370 degrees. Dredge chicken in flour, shake off excess, and place in skillet. Fry chicken on both sides until golden brown (about 4 or 5 minutes per side). Remove chicken; place on paper towel to drain.

Serves 6 to 8

This was an all-time family favorite and was served often—especially when my grandmother came to visit. When Mother fried chicken for our large family, she had to fry seven chickens. While this was unbelievable to most people, my father always said fried chicken was something you could eat, even if you were not hungry. I think people could smell that chicken all over the neighborhood—and they came from far and wide just to have a piece. When I started my own family and I made fried chicken, it brought back great memories of my youth. And while I don't fry seven chickens, I always make extra in case I have unexpected visitors. Because as my father said, "You don't have to be hungry to eat fried chicken."

Mother's Fried Chicken

New Orleans Shrimp Po Boy

New Orleans Shrimp Po Boy

2 lbs. shrimp, peeled and deveined
Salt and pepper to season
2 eggs, lightly beaten
½ cup whole milk
2 cups yellow cornmeal
2 tablespoons plain flour
1 cup vegetable oil
1 loaf French bread
Mayonnaise
Lettuce, romaine or iceberg
Tomatoes, sliced
Dill pickles, sliced

Season shrimp with salt and pepper. In a medium bowl, combine eggs and milk, beat lightly. Place cornmeal and flour in separate medium bowl and combine. Dip shrimp in egg/milk mixture then toss in cornmeal/flour mixture. Shake off excess.

In a 12-inch skillet (for best results, use a cast-iron skillet), heat oil on medium/high heat. Place shrimp into hot oil; do not overcrowd pan. Fry on both sides until golden brown, about 2 minutes per side. Remove shrimp and place on paper towel to drain.

To assemble sandwich, slice French bread lengthwise. Apply mayonnaise to taste. Generously load shrimp onto bread; then add lettuce, tomatoes, and pickles. Slice into four sections.

Makes 4 sandwiches

New Orleans Shrimp Po Boy's Story

A Po Boy is a traditional New Orleans sandwich, but it is all about French bread—the bread that makes the sandwich! In the old days, this sandwich was created because it was an inexpensive way to get a good meal. Over the years, especially in New Orleans, it has become one of the most popular things on a restaurant menu, big or small. You could even get a Po Boy at the corner grocery store. In my family, this was also a treat. When my father would bring home that hot French bread, we were always ready with great things to pile high on the sandwich. When I took my husband to New Orleans for the first time, I couldn't wait to have him experience this sandwich. I explained the term "dressed," which means lettuce, tomatoes, pickles, and mayonnaise, the traditional way to eat this great sandwich. No thanks, he said, I would like mine "naked." Just the fried shrimp. Well, I guess you can't expect everyone to embrace old traditions!

Seafood Pasta

½ cup garlic, finely chopped
¼ cup shallots, finely chopped
1 stick butter
⅓ cup extra-virgin olive oil
2 lbs. shrimp, peeled, deveined, and seasoned with salt and pepper
2 large lobster tails, cooked and cut in large pieces
½ lb. jumbo lump crabmeat
2 tablespoons ground black pepper
Juice of 1 large lemon
¼ cup finely chopped flat-leaf parsley
1 lb. cooked linguini noodles

In a large 12-inch skillet, sauté garlic and shallots in butter and olive oil about 10 minutes or until mixture is soft. Add shrimp and cook about 10 minutes or until shrimp are pink. Add lobster, crabmeat, and pepper. Cover and cook for another 10 minutes. Add lemon juice and parsley. Cover and cook an additional 5 minutes. Toss with linguini noodles.

Serves 4 to 6

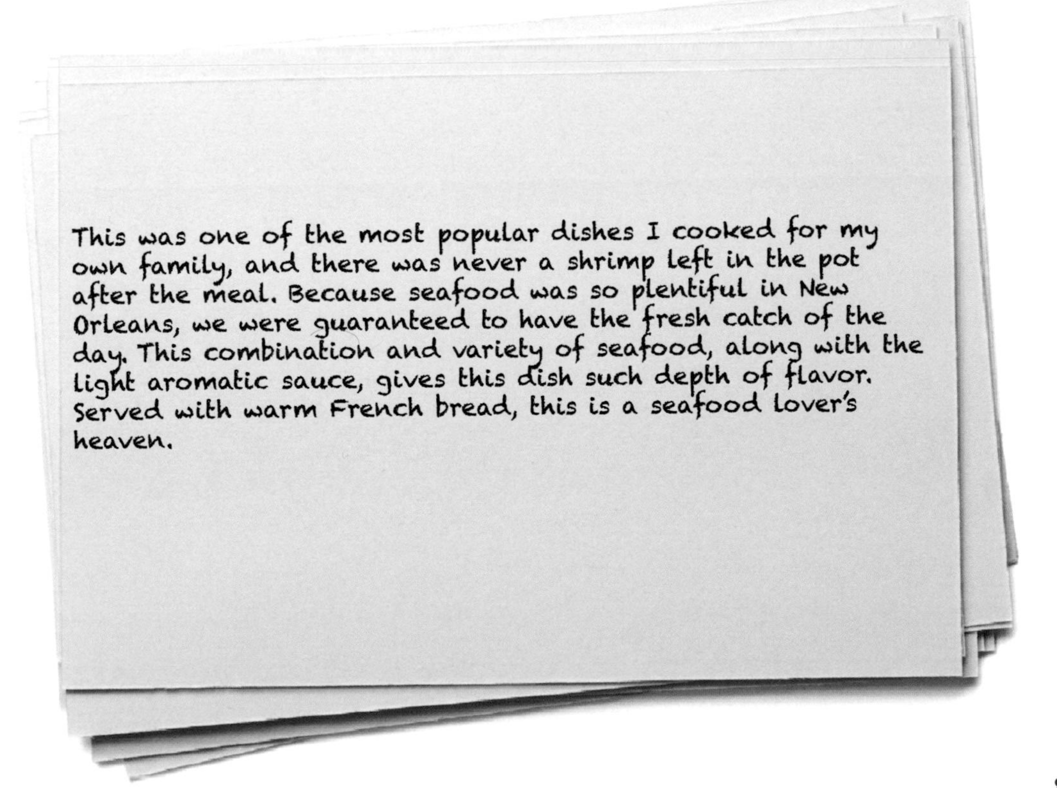

Desserts

New Orleans Bread Pudding (Served with Crème Anglaise)

1 loaf of French bread
3 (12 oz.) cans of evaporated milk
2 cups heavy whipping cream
8 eggs, lightly beaten
2 tablespoons pure vanilla bean paste
3 tablespoons pure vanilla extract
1 (15 oz.) can of fruit cocktail in heavy syrup*
1¼ cups sugar
1 cup raisins
1 cup coconut

Break French bread in small pieces and put into large bowl. Add evaporated milk and cream, and stir until all incorporated. In a separate bowl, beat eggs and add vanillas. Add mixture to bread and stir well. Add fruit cocktail (including syrup), sugar, raisins, and coconut. Stir until fully incorporated (mixture will be lumpy). Pour mixture into a 10 x 14 casserole pan, greased with butter. Put casserole into pan of water, about 1 inch from the top. Bake at 350 degrees for 1 hour 20 minutes, or until a knife comes out clean.

Serves about 10-12

* I usually take out the cherries.

Crème Anglaise

2 cups whole milk
1 egg and 4 egg yolks
¼ cup granulated sugar
1 tablespoon vanilla paste

In a small sauce pan, on medium heat, cook milk for about 2 minutes (or until milk is hot). In a small glass bowl, whisk eggs and sugar until dissolved. Add ½ of hot milk to bowl and whisk gently; add this to hot milk mixture and continue to cook. Using a wooden spoon, continue to cook mixture for 5 to 8 minutes, stirring constantly until mixture can coat the back of a spoon. Mixture will start to thicken. Add vanilla paste and gently incorporate into the mixture. Remove from heat and place in glass bowl. Let cool for 1 minute, then cover with plastic wrap. Be sure to cover the mixture so it doesn't form a skin on top of the bowl. Refrigerate until ready to use.

New Orleans Bread Pudding's Story

This is my grandmother's recipe, and a New Orleans tradition. French bread was commonly served in New Orleans, and my father would often bring home hot French bread from the bakery. The bread was so hot that the butter would melt on the bread before you could take a bite. Leftover French bread made great bread pudding, and families and restaurants all over the city prepared their version of this dessert. I think bread pudding had a special meaning for us when it was served during Christmas because it was reminiscent of my father's English heritage.

New Orleans Bread Pudding

Apple Tart

4 large Honeycrisp or Fuji Apples
1 large orange (zest and juice)
3/4 cup granulated sugar
1 tablespoon cinnamon
1 tablespoon nutmeg
1/4 teaspoon allspice
Pastry dough
1 egg plus 1 teaspoon water (egg wash for finishing)

Peel apples and cut in half. Thinly slice apples and put in large bowl. Add zest and juice from 1 large orange and toss gently. In a small bowl, combine sugar, cinnamon, nutmeg, and allspice. Add 3/4 of mixture to apples and toss gently, leaving remaining mixture for topping. Roll out pastry into a 12-inch round and place in the center of a 14 x 16 flat cookie sheet. Leaving a one-inch border between edge of dough and apples, place apples in a circle, overlapping slightly, around the entire dough. Continue with second row inside the first row of apples. Add a third smaller grouping of apples inside second circle. Turn pastry dough up and over edges of the apples, making a 1-inch crust on tart. Brush dough with egg wash and sprinkle entire tart with remaining sugar mixture. Bake at 425 degrees for 30 to 40 minutes or until pastry is golden brown.

Serves 6 to 8

Pastry Dough

3/4 stick unsalted butter
4 tablespoons shortening
1 1/2 cups all-purpose flour
1/2 teaspoon baking powder
1 teaspoon salt
2 tablespoons granulated sugar
4 tablespoons very cold water

Dice butter into small cubes and put in freezer, along with shortening. Place flour, baking powder, salt, and sugar in bowl and mix. Add butter and shortening. Using a pastry cutter, cut butter and shortening into the flour, until mixture resembles coarse crumbs. Stir in water. Immediately turn onto floured board and make a flat, round ball. Wrap in plastic wrap and refrigerate for 1 hour before using.

Apple Tart's Story

My daughters have always loved this tart. I usually make this during the Fall when the apples are crisp and firm. It's wonderful for breakfast, and when that tart is in the oven, you can smell the cinnamon throughout the house. I sometimes make this for dessert and serve it with a scoop of vanilla ice cream. When I bring this warm tart to the table, it makes such a stunning display and those apples smell so enticing.

Spice Cake

2 sticks butter (softened at room temperature)
1 cup granulated sugar
1 cup dark brown sugar
4 eggs
2 teaspoons pure vanilla extract
3 cups plain flour
2 teaspoons baking powder
1 teaspoon baking soda
1 teaspoon salt
1 tablespoon cinnamon
1 teaspoon nutmeg
½ teaspoon allspice
8 oz. sour cream
1 cup whole milk

Using a mixer on medium speed, cream butter and both sugars. Add eggs and vanilla, and beat until fully incorporated. Sift together all dry ingredients and gradually add to butter mixture, making sure everything is incorporated. Add sour cream, then slowly add milk and mix well. Pour in bundt baking pan and bake at 350 degrees for 50 minutes to 1 hour, or until toothpick comes out clean. Let cool and glaze with frosting.

Frosting:

2 cups powdered sugar
½ stick unsalted butter, softened
1 tablespoon pure vanilla extract
½ cup whole milk

Combine all ingredients using a mixer or a whisk and pour over cake.

Spice Cake's Story

On Christmas Eve, my siblings and I have always attended midnight Mass at our local Catholic church. When we came home from church, we would walk through the door of the house and were immediately hit with the smell of spice cake. We knew it was Christmas. This was a tradition at our house, but of course that cake didn't last long. Cakes disappeared fast at our house, so if you were ever offered a piece of cake, you took it! When we would have guests we made sure we instructed them in the ways of a large family. If you wait until later, it will be gone.

Lemon Cake

2 sticks butter (softened to room temperature)
2 cups sugar
4 eggs
2 teaspoons pure vanilla extract
3 cups plain flour
2 teaspoons baking powder
1 teaspoon salt
8 oz. sour cream
¾ cup whole milk
1 tablespoon lemon zest

Using a mixer on medium speed, combine butter and sugar. Add eggs and vanilla; beat until all incorporated. Sift together flour, baking powder, and salt, and gradually add to butter mixture, making sure everything is incorporated. Add sour cream. Slowly add milk and mix well. Add lemon zest.

Pour in bundt baking pan and bake at 350 degrees for 50 minutes to 1 hour, or until a toothpick comes out clean.

Lemon Topping:

½ cup sugar
Juice from 2 lemons (including pulp)
2 tablespoons lemon zest

In a small sauce pan on medium heat, combine sugar, lemon juice and lemon zest. Stirring constantly, let mixture come to a complete boil (about 5 minutes). Immediately remove from heat and cool for 1 minute. Drizzle over lemon cake.

Lemon Cake's Story

My husband says this cake is very refreshing. This was my aunt's signature dish, and one of my father's favorites. My father had a wicked sweet tooth and loved desserts. It didn't matter what he had for dinner, he was always looking for dessert after the meal. If my mother failed to make dessert, no bother, he would promptly make a trip to visit his sister, because she always made dessert. I think she made several desserts just in case he came wandering around her door in the evening. Sometimes my father would slice a little piece of cake and eat it in the car on his way home.

5 lbs. fresh peaches (ripe and semi-soft)
1 cup granulated sugar
1 cup dark brown sugar, packed
1 tablespoon cinnamon
1 tablespoon nutmeg
¼ teaspoon allspice
1 teaspoon pure vanilla extract
1 teaspoon orange zest
½ cup flour
1 tablespoon cornstarch
1 egg with 1 teaspoon water (egg wash for finishing)
1 teaspoon each of sugar, cinnamon, and nutmeg (for topping)
Pastry dough

Peel peaches, slice 1-inch thick, and put in bowl. Add sugar, brown sugar, cinnamon, nutmeg, allspice, vanilla, and orange zest. Gently mix together, then add flour and cornstarch. Pour into 13 x 9 baking pan. Roll out pastry dough to a 10 x 14 rectangle, ½-inch thick. Gently roll dough onto top of pan. Fold dough over edges of pan and crimp down, pressing gently to make it stick to the edges of pan. Brush entire dough with egg wash. Make three 2-inch slits in top of dough (to allow steam to escape). Sprinkle with remaining sugar mixture. Bake at 350 degrees for 50 minutes to 1 hour, or until crust is golden brown.

Serves 6 to 8

Pastry Dough

¾ stick unsalted butter
4 tablespoons shortening
1½ cups all-purpose flour
½ teaspoon baking powder
1 teaspoon salt
2 tablespoons granulated sugar
4 tablespoons very cold water

Dice butter into small cubes and put in freezer, along with shortening. Place flour, baking powder, salt, and sugar in bowl and mix. Add butter and shortening. Using a pastry cutter, cut butter and shortening into the flour, until mixture resembles coarse crumbs. Stir in water. Immediately turn onto floured board and make a flat, round ball. Wrap in plastic wrap and refrigerate for 1 hour before using.

Peach Cobbler's Story

This was always a summer dessert, when peaches were at their best. This was my grandmother's recipe, but I updated it with fresh ingredients and included the orange zest for added flavor. Summers in New Orleans were hot and humid, so fruit desserts were very refreshing and added a lighter end to the meal. When my grandmother made peach cobbler, she made it in the same large pan she used to cook turkey. She would bring it over to our house piping hot. We just couldn't wait to dig into those soft, tender peaches lying in a bed of spices and natural juices, covered by that light, flaky crust.

2 cups uncooked long-grain rice
1 large egg, lightly beaten
1½ cups heavy whipping cream
1 tablespoon plain flour
½ cup granulated sugar
½ cup powdered sugar
¾ cup raisins
½ teaspoon cinnamon
½ tablespoon nutmeg
¼ teaspoon salt
1 tablespoon pure vanilla extract

Using a 9-inch pot, cook rice in 6 cups of water on medium/high heat. Bring to a boil, reduce heat, and let cook for about 20 to 30 minutes until rice is fully cooked, stirring frequently. Rice will be sticky. Reduce heat to medium/low. Add egg, cream, flour, sugars, raisins, cinnamon, nutmeg, salt, and vanilla. Stir well and cook for about 10 minutes. Pour mixture in 9 x 9 casserole dish or individual serving dishes. Refrigerate for 2 hours.

Serves 4 to 6

My mother loved rice pudding. I think this became a family favorite because we always had rice; so many New Orleans dishes used rice. My dad would buy rice in a sack and we would use a measuring cup to scoop it out when we needed it. With so many kids, that sack of rice didn't last very long. I always loved rice and if there was any left over, which was not very often, I would sneak in the refrigerator and eat it cold. When my mother overcooked the rice for a meal, we knew we would be having rice pudding for dessert.

Simple Pie Crust

1½ sticks unsalted butter
⅓ cup shortening
3 cups all-purpose flour
1 teaspoon baking powder
1 teaspoon salt
¼ cup granulated sugar
⅓ cup very cold water

Dice butter into small cubes and put in freezer, along with the ⅓ cup shortening. Place flour, baking powder, salt, and sugar in bowl and mix. Add butter and shortening. Using a pastry cutter, cut butter and shortening into the flour, leaving small pieces of mixture. Stir in water. Immediately turn onto floured board and make a round, flat ball. Wrap in plastic wrap and refrigerate for 1 hour before dividing in half and rolling out into 2 round crusts.

Makes 2 (9-inch) pie crusts

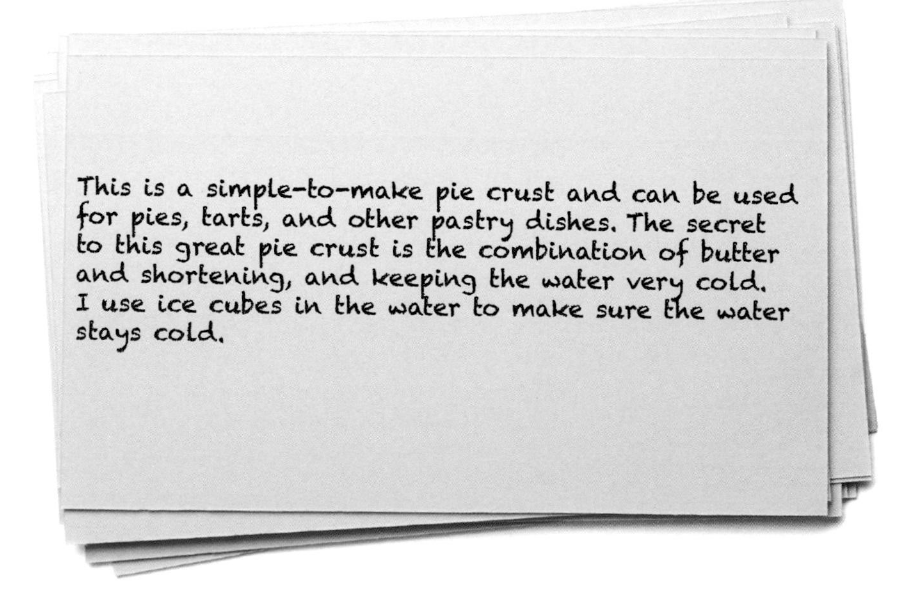

Pecan Pie

½ cup light corn syrup
½ cup dark corn syrup
3 eggs, lightly beaten
2 tablespoons butter, melted
1 tablespoon pure vanilla extract
1 teaspoon cinnamon
1 teaspoon nutmeg
1 cup chopped pecans
1 uncooked 9-inch deep dish pie crust
1 cup pecan halves (for garnishing)

Combine corn syrups, eggs, butter, vanilla, cinnamon, and nutmeg; mix well. Fold in chopped pecans. Pour mixture into pie crust. Place pecan halves on top of pie, making a circle with the pecans. Bake in oven at 350 degrees for 1 hour, or until a knife inserted in center of pie comes out clean.

Serves 6 to 8

This is a very traditional Southern dessert, and my sister Donna is our expert at making this pie. We had a pecan tree in the backyard, lots of families did. Sometimes you could hear the popping of those pecans on the roof of our house. During the summer, we would grab a bag and go out in the yard to gather as many pecans as we could. Of course, we would be eating them as we were picking them. We would have bushels of pecans and my mother would always divide the bounty and give them to friends throughout the neighborhood. They were so sweet and crunchy—a real summertime favorite.

Easy Apple Pie

5 lbs. apples, a combination of Fuji, Honeycrisp, Gala, or Golden
1 large orange (zest and juice)
½ cup plain flour
1 tablespoon cinnamon
1 tablespoon nutmeg
½ teaspoon allspice
½ cup granulated sugar
½ cup dark brown sugar
1 teaspoon salt
2 (10-inch) pie crusts
1 egg and 1 tablespoon water for egg wash

Peel and core apples then slice and place in large bowl. Add orange zest and juice and toss gently. Combine flour, cinnamon, nutmeg, allspice, sugars, and salt in a separate bowl. Add to apples and toss gently to coat entire mixture.

Roll out one pie crust and place in a 9-inch pie pan, extending the crust over the rim. Fill with apple mixture. Brush pie crust edges with egg wash—this will help cement the two crusts together. Roll out second pie crust and place on top of filling, trimming edges to about 1½ inches over the side of the pie. Crimp the two layers together with a fork. Brush the entire top pie crust with egg wash. Cut about 3 or 4 slits on top of pie to allow steam to escape.

Place pie on a cookie sheet and bake at 400 degrees for 1 to 1½ hours, or until pie crust is browned.

Serves 6 to 8

Apple Pie's Story

What seemed to come from scarce ingredients made the best tasting pie, and my daughters always loved when I made homemade Apple Pie. This was one of my specialties, and I always made it during the holidays. We started using different types of apples because we could never seem to keep apples around without them being eaten right away by my brothers and sisters. My mother would say just use a "hodgepodge" of apples, because that was what we had available. As it turned out, we thought this gave the pie more depth of flavor.

Sweet Potato Pie

Sweet Potato Pie

5 lbs whole sweet potatoes
1 stick unsalted butter
5 eggs, lightly beaten
1¼ cups granulated sugar
1 cup brown sugar, packed
1 tablespoon vanilla
1 tablespoon cinnamon
1 tablespoon nutmeg
¼ teaspoon ginger
¼ teaspoon allspice
1 cup evaporated milk
2 tablespoons plain flour
2 (9-inch) deep-dish frozen pie shells, thawed

Peel and dice sweet potatoes, place in pot with water (covering all the potatoes with water), and boil until potatoes are soft (about 30 to 45 minutes). Drain water and place potatoes in large bowl. Add butter and mash until potatoes are completely soft and mixed with the butter. Add eggs, sugar, and brown sugar, and mix well. Add vanilla, cinnamon, nutmeg, ginger, and allspice, incorporating well into the potatoes. Slowly add evaporated milk and mix well, then add flour. Mixture may be slightly lumpy; make sure all ingredients are incorporated well.

Pour about one-fourth of the mixture into a blender. Using the "blend" button, blend for about 1 minute, or until mixture is completely smooth. Pour mixture into unbaked pie shell. Add another fourth of mixture to blender, blend and pour into pie shell. Continue processing one-fourth of the mixture until all mixture is blended and poured into second pie shell.

Place pies on a cookie sheet and bake at 375 degrees for about 1 hour. Check center of pie to make sure they are done. Cool and serve.

Each pie serves 6 to 8

Sweet Potato Pie's Story

My sisters and I perfected this recipe over the years, and my sister El makes this more than anyone. While my mother insisted we have pumpkin pie at Thanksgiving, we always had sweet potato pie as well. I think the reason this pie was so popular in my family was because it had a lighter texture than pumpkin pie. The combination of spices and the fresh ingredients made this dish a special treat that we made all year long.

2½ cups plain flour
1½ teaspoons baking powder
Pinch of salt
1 cup unsalted butter, room temperature
1½ cups granulated sugar
2 large eggs
1 tablespoon vanilla extract

Sift flour, baking powder, and salt together and put aside. In a large bowl, cream butter and sugar. Lightly beat eggs and add vanilla. Add this mixture to butter and sugar, and mix well. Add dry ingredients to mixture (add ⅓ at a time). Mix well, cover with plastic wrap, and refrigerate for 2 hours. Roll out dough, cut cookies. Bake cookies at 425 degrees for about 12 to 15 minutes.

Makes 3 dozen cookies

Every year at Christmas, I made these cookies with my daughters. It became my family's tradition on Christmas Eve to make these wonderful, buttery cookies. We made them the old-fashioned way by rolling out the dough and using cookie cutters to make festive holiday decorations. We would sprinkle the cookies with colorful sugar confections and bake them until they were golden brown. When my daughters were little, I think we got more sugar on the floor than the cookies, but it was always so much fun. Even today, Eve and Mia look forward to making Christmas cookies during the holidays, and I love sharing that special time with them each year.

Banana Fritters

2 cups plain flour
¼ cup granulated sugar (plus extra sugar for topping)
1 tablespoon baking powder
1 teaspoon salt
1½ cups whole milk
2 eggs, lightly beaten
1 tablespoon vanilla extract
2 cups chopped bananas (or 3 small bananas)
¼ cup vegetable oil

Using a large bowl, combine flour, sugar, baking powder, and salt. Add milk, eggs, and vanilla and stir well. Fold in bananas. Using an 11-inch skillet, heat oil on high heat. Pour a spoonful of mixture (about 4 x 4 inches) into skillet. Cook until edges turn brown. Flip and cook on the other side. Remove fritter and place on paper towel to drain. Sprinkle with sugar.

Serves 8 to 10

My mother loved bananas. While we rarely had fruit left in the house, when we did, she would make these wonderful banana fritters. We always got our fruit from a guy driving around through the neighborhood in his truck. Bananas were relatively inexpensive, so my mother always bought a bushel of them. Banana fritters were a real treat, served with sprinkled sugar on top instead of syrup.
The size of the fritters was always smaller than pancakes. That just meant we could eat more of them.

Banana Fritters

How to Form Calas (Rice Cakes)

Calas (Creole French Rice Cakes)

2 cups long grain white rice
1 cup plain flour
1 tablespoon baking powder
1½ cups granulated sugar
1 teaspoon salt
1 egg, lightly beaten
1 tablespoon vanilla extract
1 quart vegetable oil
1 cup powdered sugar (for garnish)

Cook rice in 6 cups of water for 30 to 35 minutes or until rice absorbs water and becomes soft. Remove and let cool for 15 minutes. Combine rice, flour, baking powder, sugar, salt, egg, and vanilla. Mix well. Let mixture rest for 30 minutes. In a deep 11-inch fry pan, preheat oil to 370 degrees. Using a 3-inch spoon, scoop rice mixture and shape calas in spoon. Using another 3-inch spoon, slide mixture into oil. Cook calas for about 2 minutes then flip over to cook the other side until golden brown. Remove from oil, place on paper towels to drain. Sprinkle with powdered sugar.

Makes 2 to 3 dozen

So many New Orleans Creole families made their version of calas. My mother said calas were the Creole version of beignets. In the old days, Creole women would sell calas on the streets of New Orleans—"Belles calas, touts chaudes!" or "Calas, very hot!" they would say. We rarely had calas; they were made only on very special occasions, but we always had them during Mardi Gras. My grandmother and aunt would make these and bring them to our house early Mardi Gras morning. The only other time I can remember having calas was when someone in our family made their First Communion (maybe a New Orleans Catholic tradition). This was an old custom in our family, and we savored calas every time they were made.

New Orleans French Rice Cakes

Recipe Index

Italicized numbers indicate photos.

Recipe Title Index

Italicized numbers indicate photos.